BOOMERANG!

Susan K. Hom

STERLING INNOVATION
New York

STERLING INNOVATION
New York

An Imprint of Sterling Publishing
387 Park Avenue South
New York, NY 10016

For Ken and Linda

STERLING, the Sterling logo, STERLING INNOVATION, and the Sterling Innovation logo are
registered trademarks of Sterling Publishing Co., Inc.

10 9 8 7 6 5 4 3 2

Published by Sterling Publishing Co., Inc.
387 Park Avenue South, New York, NY 10016
© 2011 by Sterling Publishing Co., Inc.
Distributed in Canada by Sterling Publishing
c/o Canadian Manda Group, 165 Dufferin Street
Toronto, Ontario, Canada M6K 3H6
Distributed in the United Kingdom by GMC Distribution Services
Castle Place, 166 High Street, Lewes, East Sussex, England BN7 1XU
Distributed in Australia by Capricorn Link (Australia) Pty. Ltd.
P.O. Box 704, Windsor, NSW 2756, Australia

This book is part of *Boomerang: Learn to Throw Like a Pro* and is not to be sold separately.

Sterling ISBN 978-1-4027-8020-2

For information about custom editions, special sales, premium
and corporate purchases, please contact Sterling Special Sales
Department at 800-805-5489 or specialsales@sterlingpublishing.com.

WARNING: Boomerangs can be dangerous. Use only in open spaces clear of
other people and property, pets or other animals.
Do not attempt to catch the boomerang as injury may occur.

DISCLAIMER: Publisher will not be liable for any injury or damage resulting in the use or misuse of the product.

CONTENTS

INTRODUCTION
The Joy of Boomerang Throwing

A baseball has *nothing* on the boomerang. Sure, it can move fast, but ultimately, it goes up, makes an arc, and then comes down. A boomerang quickly spins in the air like a rotating propeller. Then it makes a graceful turn and hovers *back* to you.

When it comes back to your hand for the first time, it feels pretty amazing. Don't worry! With some practice, you'll get the hang of it. If you take the basic form of the overhand throw and add a snap of your wrist, you'll be able to launch your boomerang into the air.

Perhaps you're looking for a new hobby—something fun to do outdoors on the weekends. Or maybe you enjoy playing sports. You'd like to try your hand at a unique set of skills: reading the wind, finding the ideal layover (launch angle), and adding just the right amount of spin to your throw. Once you've learned the basics, boomerang throwing can be a satisfying hobby or a challenging competitive sport.

You'll be in good company, too. Boomerang throwing has grown into a popular sport in the United States since the late 1960s, thanks to an influential article published by *Scientific American* in 1968 and to the annual Smithsonian Boomerang Tournament, organized by Ben Ruhe, which started the following year. Today there are hundreds of thousands of recreational throwers in this country, according to the United States Boomerang Association (USBA).

It's also a competitive sport around the world. There's even a World Boomerang Championship, which is held every two years and is comprised of nationally ranked athletes competing as individuals and on teams. They represent more than a dozen countries, including Australia, France, Germany, Japan, Switzerland, and the United States.

In these pages, you'll discover the fascinating world of the boomerang, which dates back to its humble beginnings as a returning stick used to hunt ducks. If you're curious about what forces are at work to make a boomerang return, check out Chapter 2. This book also includes information on getting out into the boomerang community with clubs, competitions, and websites. So without further ado, let's get your boomerang into the air and back into your hands.

CHAPTER 1

It's Flight Time!

Like any sport, boomerang throwing requires practice and patience. Here's the good news: you don't have to be extremely strong. You've got to go with the flow. Sometimes you'll need to make adjustments to your layover depending on the direction of the wind. With a little bit of hardness and, most importantly, spin to your throw, your boomerang will return to you.

Don't worry if it doesn't come back to you on your first day out. Check out the troubleshooting section later in this chapter for more specific advice. Once you've gotten your boomerang to fly in a full circle, you'll start catching it. Then you can work on improving your technique and also try out some of the trick catches and games described in this chapter.

Safety Tips

Before you launch your boomerang into the air, check out these important safety tips. A boomerang's unique ability to return sets it apart from a baseball or Frisbee. So you need to always be aware of the people and objects around you.

1. Great flying weather is when there is only a little breeze. The wind is usually calm in the early morning or before sunset.
2. Choose a large practice area. Ideal spots are an empty, grassy field or a football field. Allow yourself a radius of about 100 yards (about 91 meters) around you because your boomerang may fly out farther than you anticipate. You'll also have better luck in getting it to return since there aren't any nearby trees to change the airflow.
3. Avoid crowded areas and fragile objects. You don't want to accidentally hit someone or break a window.
4. If people stop to watch, give them the heads-up that they need to pay attention to the flight of your boomerang to avoid any accidents.

5. Protect your eyes and hands by wearing safety goggles and gloves.
6. *Never* throw your boomerang to someone. If you want to play catch with a friend, stick with a Frisbee or baseball.
7. Don't throw your boomerang in a sideways motion, like you would with a Frisbee. This will cause the boomerang to swoop wildly.
8. Catch your boomerang when it's about level to your chest or even lower. Use a sandwich clap (see page 14) with flat palms. The wings are spinning very quickly, so don't try to grab it by one of its wingtips.
9. If children want to try some practice throws, tell them to wait until you're available to supervise.
10. Stick with the enclosed beginner-level boomerang until you have more experience. Sharpen your throwing and catching skills before you progress to a fast-moving, competition-level boomerang. Since advanced boomerangs can cover longer distances, you'll need to find a larger field.

A Note for Left-Handed Throwers

The boomerang that comes with this book is for a right-handed thrower. If you're a left-handed thrower, you will need to buy a *left-handed boomerang*. Check out the Boomerang Man website or the USBA website for a list of vendors. (See the website list on page 46.)

A left-handed boomerang circles in a clockwise direction, whereas a right-handed boomerang circles in a counterclockwise direction. The instructions in this book are written with a right-handed thrower in mind. If you're throwing with your left hand, just reverse the direction.

The Parts of a Boomerang

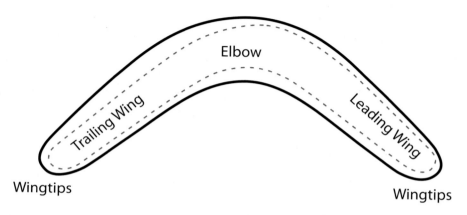

Elbow

Trailing Wing

Leading Wing

Wingtips

Wingtips

Here's a close-up look at a boomerang. The shape of a boomerang wing is similar to that of an airplane wing. They are both airfoils. When it travels, the air above the wing moves faster than the air below the wing because of the curved top. The air above has a longer distance to travel. The faster air results in a lower pressure above when compared to that below the wing. This difference in pressure is the reason the wing *lifts* up. We'll talk more about lift and aerodynamic forces in Chapter 2.

Leading Wing: First wing to slice through the air when the boomerang is rotating. Its edge is called the leading edge.
Trailing Wing: This wing "trails behind" the leading wing during the boomerang's rotation in the air. Its edge is called the trailing edge.
Elbow: Curved joint that connects the boomerang's wings.
Wingtips: Ends of the boomerang.

Checklist for Throwing and Catching Your Boomerang

Before we go into more detail about how to make a successful throw, here are a few simple steps to keep in mind.

1. Hold your boomerang by the leading or trailing wing. Pinch your boomerang wing with your thumb and forefinger. Another way is to wrap your fingers around the bottom of the wing as if you were gripping a hammer. Keep the unpainted, flat side away from you.

2. Aim to launch it at an angle between 10 to 30 degrees from an imaginary vertical line to the ground, at a point above the horizon, such as a line of distant treetops. Cock the boomerang back over your shoulder.

3. Imagine that you're going to crack a whip. Step into an overhand throw with your left foot. Release the boomerang vertically in a hard throw with a little spin.

4. As your boomerang hovers on its return path, wait for it to drop to chest level or below. Catch your boomerang's elbow using a sandwich clap with flat palms. Keep your fingers stiff. As you finish the clap, draw your arms inward.

The Comfortable Grip

As you can see, your boomerang has two sides: one that is curved and painted and one that is flat and plain. When holding your boomerang, keep its flat side away from your body. You can hold either the leading or trailing wing.

There are two types of grips. The first type is pinching the boomerang between your thumb and forefinger. This is called the pinch grip. When you snap your wrist, you give the boomerang its spin.

The other option is the cradle or wraparound grip. Hold the boomerang with its flat side facing your palm and wrap your fingers around the bottom of the wing as if you were gripping a hammer.

Go ahead and try out both grips. Here are two things to keep in mind when choosing a grip: Which one feels more comfortable? Which one gives you more spin and more control when you throw?

"What I like best about boomerang throwing is that it's both very precise and yet imprecise, since it's wind dependent. You have to feel the wind, and the way it shifts. There's also the feeling of making the perfect throw."

—Richard Bower, member of the U.S. Team Rad Revolution, winner of the 2010 World Boomerang Championship

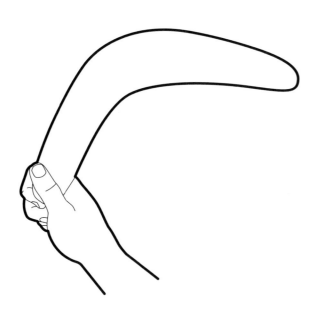

Pinch Grip

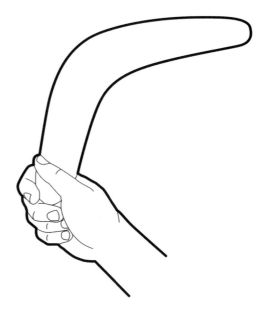

Cradle Grip

The Throw

To remember the five elements of a successful throw, keep in mind this acronym—WELSH—created by Pat Steigman. It stands for Wind, Elevation, Layover, Spin, and Hardness.

Wind

First you need to determine the direction of the wind. Face the wind and then slowly turn to the right. Picture a clock's hands at two o'clock and turn at about that angle. You should feel the wind on your left cheek. You'll be throwing to the right of the wind. The wind is constantly shifting, and in many different ways, too. The direction of the wind is one of the variable factors in boomerang throwing. It's hard to predict what the wind will do. But with more experience, you'll sharpen your instincts about the different ways the wind can shift and keep that in mind when you set up your throw.

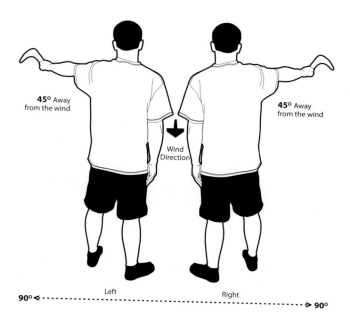

45° Away from the wind

45° Away from the wind

Wind Direction

Left

Right

90°◀ ┈┈┈┈┈┈┈┈┈┈┈┈┈┈┈┈┈┈┈┈ ▶ **90°**

Elevation

You'll release your boomerang at eye level and about ten degrees above the ground. Find a focal point above the horizon, such as a line of treetops in the distance.

Layover

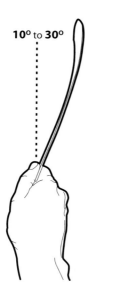

10° to 30°

Hold up your boomerang so that it's perpendicular to the ground. Now *slightly* tilt it from this imaginary vertical line at an angle between 10 to 30 degrees, which is its layover. Picture the face of a clock and the numbers twelve and one. The layover should be between twelve o'clock and one o'clock. It's a very small angle. You don't need a lot of layover.

   Cock the boomerang back over your shoulder. Your elbow should be bent. Imagine that you're going to crack a whip. At the end of the throwing motion, your arm will be extended with your hand at eye level.

Spin

Step into an overhand throw with your left foot. Don't throw it sideways like a Frisbee. Resist the urge to let go of the boomerang. To get spin, hold the boomerang tightly until it feels like it's pulling itself away from your grip. Throw it straight and above the shoulder. Release your boomerang vertically.

Hardness

No wimpy throws allowed. A good motto is: throw it like you mean it. But don't go overboard. Often a beginner's throws are "all arm." Instead, focus on getting more spin rather than throwing harder.

The Catch

After your boomerang has consistently returned, you can practice your catches. As your boomerang hovers on its return path, get into position so that it will be at about the level of your chest or even lower. Hold your hands one over the other about 18 inches (46 centimeters) apart. Catch your boomerang's elbow using a sandwich clap with flat palms. Keep your fingers stiff. As you finish the clap, draw your arms inward.

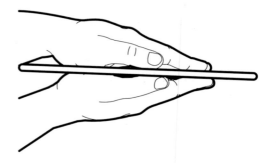

Remember that the wings are spinning very quickly, so don't try to grab it by one of its wingtips. If it's coming toward you too fast, duck or move out of the way. But keep an eye on it, because it may come back in a loop if it doesn't hit something else first.

Making a Clunker

If you want to fly your boomerang in heavy wind conditions, you can change it into a clunker, a boomerang with airfoils. You can add coins to your boomerang's wings to allow the boomerang to fly with less lift. When you tape dimes, nickels, or quarters (or other coins) on the underside of one or both wings, you can change the way your boomerang flies. If you place the weights near the wingtips, your boomerang will fly a greater distance. You can create more spin by placing the coins near the elbow.

Wind foilers are flaps made out of aluminum foil tape. Cut a piece of tape 2 inches (5 centimeters) long. Bend the tape so that it's about ¼ inch (6 millimeters) high. You simply place the wind foiler on your boomerang's leading wing near the wingtip. You can bend the flap when there is less wind.

Advanced-Level Throws

Once you get the hang of the boomerang throw, here are two advanced-level throws. Doubling is a technique done in competitions. It's part of the second half of the Trick Catch/Doubling event. (You can read more about Trick Catch/Doubling in Chapter 4.) You'll need two boomerangs for this type of throw. You can also try throwing your boomerang while holding its elbow. Be sure to give it some spin.

Doubling
When you have more experience, try throwing two boomerangs at the same time from one hand. The best way to keep your boomerangs from colliding in midair is to hold them tightly by the wingtips. Just as you're about to release the boomerangs, give them a tight squeeze to separate them.

Elbow Launch

A pinch grip works best with an elbow launch. To gain maximum spin, make sure the boomerang is cocked back in your hand and snap your wrist like you mean it.

Trick Catches

The two things you want to master before you attempt trick catches are: a consistent throw (one where your boomerang returns the same way each time) and a consistent two-handed catch. Just keep practicing in the same place until the motion becomes familiar.

When doing trick catches, keep this goal in mind: anticipate where your boomerang is going to be and get in front of it. Your boomerang is traveling in a forward direction, but also spinning. You'll need to watch the forward path of the boomerang to adjust your position. The more time you spend with your boomerang, the more you'll be able to anticipate its location and know how much time you have to get ready to catch it.

Right- or Left-Hand Clean (One-Handed Catch)

The two most important things to keep in mind when making a right- or left-hand clean is, first, only catch it if it's coming toward you slowly, and second, stay focused on your boomerang when you catch it. Don't close your eyes or look away. When your boomerang falls to about shoulder level, bend your elbow and stretch your hand out so that your palm is facing up. Don't hesitate when you go for your one-handed catch, because once you touch it, your boomerang will sharply change the direction of its path.

Two-Hand-Behind-the-Back

Anticipate where the boomerang will fall in relation to your hip. Position yourself in front of the boomerang. When your boomerang is at eye level, pivot and make a two-handed catch.

Two-Hand-Under-the-Leg

Lift your left leg high so that you can catch your boomerang from below. You'll catch it when it drops to the height of your knee. Your right arm will be stretched out, so your right hand is ready to catch it with the left. When you're comfortable with either two-handed catch, you can try catching it under your leg with one hand.

Foot Catch

Watch your boomerang and time it so that you'll have enough time to get on the ground. In a sitting position, make a sandwich clap using your feet, with one leg above the other. You may need to lean over on your side to catch it.

Freestyling

How flexible are you? Here's one way to find out. Just like the freestyle moves used with a Frisbee, you can try to twist, jump, or somersault in the air while catching your boomerang.

Juggling

It's important to use two boomerangs with the same flight path for this trick, so that you can consistently release your boomerang from the same point. Also, these boomerangs should be able to hover for a long time so that you'll be able to get in a ready position for your catch.

You'll have to multitask a throw with a catch. Make sure that the incoming boomerang is in front of you. Throw the second boomerang into the air. You'll need lots of patience for juggling. Juggling challenges your hand–eye coordination and your ability to read the shifts in the wind. It's very hard to master, but it can be fun once you get the hang of it.

Trick Catch Games

Here are some fun trick catch games to try out with other players and their boomerangs. "Hackuracy" uses the painted concentric circles found in a boomerang competition field. You can play the other games in your usual practice area.

Cauliflower

All of the players simultaneously throw their boomerangs up in the air while one person names a trick catch for the group to perform. Continue to play with a new caller.

G-L-O-R-P

If you like the basketball game H-O-R-S-E, you'll enjoy this freestyle game. Create a lineup of players. The Dominator (first person to throw) does a trick catch (any kind is okay except a two-handed catch). If the Dominator makes a successful catch, then each of the other players take turns doing the same catch. If one of them misses, that player is assigned a letter. During the course of the game, for each failed catch the player acquires a letter: G, L, O, R. After a player gets the letter P, he or she is out of the game.

The Dominator can't do the same trick catch twice in a row. A "pass" is when the Dominator makes a two-handed catch or flubs the trick catch but luckily doesn't drop it. Now the other players take turns doing the same trick catch. If the next player drops the catch, that person gets a letter. However, if the player makes the trick catch, that person becomes the next Dominator.

The Dominator continues to choose the trick catches until dropping a catch. Then the next player in the line becomes the Dominator. The new Dominator isn't allowed to do the same trick catch that the last Dominator just performed. The last person left is the winner.

Hackuracy

In the competition event Accuracy (described in Chapter 4), there are five concentric circles painted on the ground with the point values spaced 2 meters (about six and a half feet) apart. The center circle has a value of 10 points, and each circle decreases in value by 2 points. The outermost circle is worth 2 points. Each player tries to get the most hackys possible before the boomerang lands inside one of the circles. A hacky catch with a boomerang is similar to bouncing a hacky sack off your leg or other body part and catching it. The player's score equals the number of hackys multiplied by the value of the Accuracy circle.

Humpty

In this game, the player makes as many throws and catches as possible with one foot planted on the ground. Only pivoting is allowed.

Team Hacky Catch

Divide into teams with four or more teammates. The first player makes a throw while the other teammates try to keep the boomerang up in the air with as many hacky moves as they can before someone catches it. The thrower isn't allowed to make the first hacky. Also, a player can't do two hackys in a row.

> **1 point:** Catch with no hacky
> **2 points:** Trick catch with no hacky
> **4 points:** Hacky and catch
> **5 points:** Hacky with trick catch
> **1 point:** Each extra hacky

Sprinkler Head

Players throw their boomerangs and try to make catches that are close to the Center of the Universe (a sprinkler head or other small object on the ground). They can throw from any location on the field. The closest catch in a round is awarded 1 point. A catch on the Center of the Universe gets 3 points. The winner is the first one to get 10 points.

Taking Care of Your Boomerang

Avoid getting your wooden boomerang wet because it will be too heavy to fly well. Moisture can cause the wood of a boomerang to warp, so keep an eye out for up or down warps, which can affect your boomerang's flight. For optimum performance, your boomerang must be flat.

You should routinely check your boomerang for flatness. Place the boomerang on a table with its curved side facing up and the wings pointing away from you. When you press down on the elbow, are the tips about ⅛ to ¼ inch (3 to 6 millimeters) off the table? Are the tips also parallel to the table? If so, then your boomerang is flat.

Continue checking its flatness by pressing down on the elbow with one finger. With your other hand, tap both wingtips. Listen for a click when you tap the middle of the wing; this means there is a down warp on the wing. If the click is lower on the wing, then your boomerang has an up warp. Don't worry about a slight up warp on the wingtip.

You can tune your wooden boomerang by heating it for a few seconds over an electric burner. First wrap the section in a wet paper towel strip, about 2 by 6 inches (5 by 15 centimeters) long. Then cover the paper towel with tin foil and bend the edges upward. This will allow the water vapor to move away from the wingtip. Apply heat about 1 inch (2.5 centimeters) above the electric burner for about 30 seconds. You'll see steam rise out of the foil. The wet paper towel and foil will protect your boomerang's wood from scorching. By warming up the glue within your boomerang, the area that you're working on will become more flexible. Add pressure in the opposite direction of the warp and keep it in that position while it sets and cools. Do this carefully to avoid breaking your boomerang. Once again, check for flatness. If you routinely check it for flatness, you'll have better flying days with your boomerang.

Word Origin

"Boomerang" comes from the word *bumerang*, which was created by the former Tharawal and Daruk tribes of New South Wales. The colonists used this word for both throwing sticks and returning boomerangs, since they incorrectly assumed the objects were one and the same. Today a boomerang is also called a *rang*, *boom*, or *returner*.

Troubleshooting

Here are the most common problems for beginner throwers and some suggestions to deal with them. Keep practicing and have fun! You can do it.

- The boomerang won't turn, and hits the ground: Give it more spin; or perhaps you're holding it upside down.
- It lands short: Throw more left of the wind.
- It lands behind you: Throw more right of the wind.
- It flies high but then crashes when it returns: You need to throw lower.
- It flies toward you but hits the ground: You need to throw harder and with more spin.

- It flies toward you but then goes over your head: You're throwing too hard.

- It flies steeply, stops, and crashes: Use less layover. Don't throw it sideways or across your body. Also check the boomerang for warps. (See "Taking Care of Your Boomerang" on page 20.)

CHAPTER 2

Why Does a Boomerang Return?

You've witnessed your boomerang's flight pattern: vertical launch, spin, turn, and hover. You've heard your boomerang's wings make a *fft, fft, fft* noise as it zips through the air. But what's going on here?

Lift of the Wings

First you make an overhand throw and release your boomerang vertically, imparting a little bit of spin. You've transferred energy to the boomerang so that it starts to spin. Its wings are slicing the air as it travels.

In the previous chapter, we mentioned that the wings are airfoils, just like an airplane's wings. Their shapes are similar. They both have a curved top and flat bottom. Air moves over them in similar ways.

Let's look at one wing. Air is fluidly traveling over the top and the bottom of the wing and meeting up at the back. However, in the same amount of time, the air on top of the wing has to travel faster than the air on the bottom of the wing because of the curved top. The air on top has a longer distance to travel. Based on Bernoulli's equation, which describes the flow of fluids, since the speed of the air's flow increases, this will cause the pressure to decrease. The relatively faster moving air results in a lower pressure on top when compared to the bottom of the wing. This difference in pressure is the reason why the wing *lifts* up.

The Turn

Your boomerang is now spinning due to the length of the wings and the angle between them. This is called *gyroscopic stability*. At a particular moment, one wing is on the top of its arc. It's spinning, and it's moving *away* from you. The other wing is also spinning, and it's moving *toward* you. Therefore, the wing on the top of the arc is relatively faster than the wing on the bottom. The difference in the velocity between the two wings results in a difference in lift. The forward-moving wing has a greater lift than the retreating wing.

Remember that the boomerang is spinning on an axis. The force that you apply to the boomerang when you launch it into the air makes the boomerang turn left, perpendicular to the path of your right-handed throw. This is called *gyroscopic precession*. The force reacts 90 degrees to the point of the applied force of your throw. So instead of continuing in a straight path, your boomerang returns to you.

The Hover

When you threw your boomerang, you applied a maximum amount of force. However, over time your boomerang loses its momentum. After it left your hand, it flew straight because of the two forces: forward velocity and gyroscopic stability. The boomerang's forward velocity starts to decrease to the point where the force of gyroscopic precession is greater, so the boomerang turns.

Since you threw your boomerang with slight layover, the boomerang lays down as it's turning. You can control the duration of your boomerang's flight by the amount of power and spin you put into your throw. That's why you want to throw your boomerang like you mean it and with plenty of spin. Ultimately, your boomerang slows down due to the force of drag, as well as the effect of gravity. As it comes toward you, it drops to a horizontal hover.

A Boomerang in Space

In 2008, Japanese astronaut Takao Doi did a fun, informal experiment with a paper boomerang in the International Space Station. World boomerang champion Yasuhiro Togai wondered how a boomerang would fly in zero gravity, so he gave Doi the paper boomerang and taught him some basic throwing skills.

Earlier in this chapter, we saw how the forces of gyroscopic stability and gyroscopic precession affect the boomerang's flight. The boomerang's ability to turn has nothing to do with gravity. So when Doi threw the boomerang in an environment with zero gravity, it returned to him, the same way it would have done on Earth.

However, the boomerang would have acted differently if Doi had thrown it outside the space station, where there is an absence of aerodynamic forces. The boomerang would have traveled straight unless it hit another object or if the Earth's gravity changed its path.

Boomerang Theories

Inventor Sir Thomas Mitchell, from New South Wales, challenged the science world with his lecture on the similarities between a boomerang and a ship's propeller in 1851.

Tips for Buying a Boomerang

If you want to buy another boomerang, especially for competitions, you should make sure that it fits the standards set by the USBA. You want a reliable boomerang that actually comes back to you. If you live near a kite specialty store, you can check out their boomerangs. Otherwise, you can look at the Boomerang Man website and the vendors section on the USBA website for a list of vendors' contact information and websites. (See the website list on page 46.) Here are some things to consider before buying a boomerang:

Left-Handed Boomerangs

If you're a left-handed thrower, you'll need to buy a left-handed boomerang. Check out the Boomerang Man website or the USBA website for a list of vendors.

Level of Experience

Stick with a beginner-level boomerang until you've been consistent with your throws and catches. After that's the case, then try throwing an intermediate level. There's nothing wrong with throwing a beginner level if you're new to the sport.

Function

Are you going to use it for a specific competition event like Maximum Time Aloft (MTA)? If so, you'll need a light and thin boomerang, which is designed specifically for MTA. On the other end of the spectrum, if you want a long-distance boomerang, you'll want to buy one that's made of more dense material.

Airfoils

Closely examine the shape of the wings. Does each wing have a curved top and flat bottom? Also check that the edges are rounded.

Warps

Make sure that there are no warps. The boomerang should lie perfectly flat on a table. (See "Taking Care of Your Boomerang" in Chapter 1 for advice on checking for flatness.)

Comfort

How does it feel in your hand? Is it too big? If it's too heavy, choose one that's lighter.

Color

Do you think it's a color that you would be able to spot easily when it's in flight? You don't want to spend most of your practice time looking for your lost boomerang. Where's the fun in that?

Your Throwing Technique and Science Go Hand in Hand

Now that you've seen how a boomerang works, you can understand why adding a little bit of layover, hardness, and especially spin is so important. You need to give your boomerang a strong applied force to set it along its elliptical path. A boomerang's aerodynamic design is truly amazing!

Boomerang Shapes

Although many modern boomerangs are shaped in a V, there are also boomerangs with multiple arms (like the tri-blader). Many boomerangs are named after their shapes, like the omega, the admiral's hat (variation of the omega), the hockey stick (an MTA boomerang in an L shape), the hook, the pinwheel, the running man (tri-blader with wavy arms), and the snake.

CHAPTER 3

Returning Sticks

Many cultures around the world used throwing sticks for hunting. These sticks were discovered in places as different as the tomb of King Tutankhamun and the Olazowa Cave in Poland (dated at 23,000 years). Throwing sticks were the precursors to boomerangs. They were a refined design of the wooden club with a curved shape and a sharp edge. Throwing sticks were large—some were 3 feet (91 centimeters) wide—and could be thrown into groups of large animals, or human enemies, from a safe distance. They were mostly used in wide-open spaces. However, throwing sticks lacked the boomerang's elbow and wings, so they were nonreturning sticks. Technically, since they only flew straight, they weren't boomerangs.

As we learned in the previous chapter, the boomerang has a unique design. It's made up of two wings connected at an angle, which is usually between 105 to 110 degrees. The wings are like the airfoils of an airplane, with a curved top and a flat bottom. The airfoils are moving forward but also spinning. The difference in the velocity between the two wings results in a difference in lift. The force that you apply to the boomerang when you launch it into the air makes the boomerang turn.

A Versatile Tool

In Australia, Aborigines created wooden boomerangs (returning sticks) with many functions in mind. They used them for sporting competitions, hunting ducks and fish, and as musical instruments during rituals.

Early Boomerang Sports

Aborigines used the returning stick in a competition where a player tried to perform a maximum number of throws before it landed in a circle marked on the ground or hit a peg. This is in the same spirit as today's competition events, which test accuracy.

In the Boulia region of South West Queensland, the tribe members created a game in which one thrower would throw the returning boomerang over a line of several players with their hands resting on each other's shoulders. The players in line would try not to get hit while the thrower tried to hit the most people with the boomerang. Each would take a turn to get the highest number of hits.

Aborigines were also fascinated by the boomerang's unique elliptical flight path. They played other games that showcased the boomerang's ability to fly in various loops.

Miniature Boomerangs

Aboriginal youngsters used miniature returning boomerangs for competition. Accounts written by early settlers describe a nighttime event where adults and children set the ends of returning boomerangs on fire before launching the spinning "fireworks" into the sky. Children also enjoyed making their own boomerangs from bark.

Hunting Waterbirds

Aboriginal people living in the southeastern region of Australia used boomerangs to scare ducks right into their nets. The ducks mistook a hovering boomerang for a predator like a hawk. In an attempt to escape, they would fly low and then would be captured, either hit by a club or trapped in a net that was set up across the water.

Commemorative Boomerang

In 1969, Australian Television Network Channel 7 gave NASA astronaut Michael Collins a boomerang in honor of the *Apollo 11* Moon landing. The boomerang represented the first man-made aerodynamic shape. You can see it on display at the Smithsonian National Air and Space Museum in Washington, DC.

Fish-Killing Boomerangs

Some Aborigines hunted for fish in tidal pools using boomerangs with sharp edges designed to cut through water. This rare fish-killing boomerang was only used in the Broome region of northwestern Australia and in Port Lincoln, part of the west coast of South Australia, because of the areas' daily tidal variations.

Boomerangs in Rituals

Boomerangs were used in ceremonial dances and as percussion instruments in ceremonies. Aborigines kept the beat with boomerangs by hitting them on the ground or rattling a pair together. Sometimes a boomerang was rubbed against another one like a bow. These boomerang instruments are still used in Aboriginal music today in central and northern Australia.

Time-Freezing Boomerang

In 1965, the Australian television show *The Magic Boomerang* debuted. It was about a boy who kept getting into trouble. But whenever he threw his time-freezing boomerang, everything around him would stop during the time of its flight. So he always had enough time to escape. The show ran for two seasons.

The Popularity of Boomerangs

Many written accounts by Europeans in the nineteenth century confused throwing sticks with returning boomerangs. They assumed that the large sticks thrown in the air to hunt large animals and wound enemies in battle were the same thing as the smaller returning kind. The earliest European description of a returning boomerang was found in the journal of Francis Louis Barrallier, which was written in 1802. Barrallier was a member of the New South Wales Corps.

Two years later, more Europeans witnessed demonstrations of the returning boomerang in Sydney. In the 1830s, travelers brought boomerangs to Dublin. It didn't take long for boomerang throwing to become popular in Europe, especially among university students in Dublin and England.

In the twentieth century, boomerangs became a part of pop culture, from symbols in Australian advertising and European postcards to props in American movies, such as the 1966 comedy *How to Steal a Million*, starring Peter O'Toole and Audrey Hepburn. The boomerang was also featured as an Australian military emblem in World War I. The symbol had a dual meaning: the boomerang was a well-known weapon, but it also represented the country's hope that their servicemen would safely return home. The boomerang is a historical symbol of Aboriginal culture and a national symbol for Australia, as well as a nostalgic icon in Western pop culture.

CHAPTER 4

The Sport of Boomerang Throwing

Now that you've discovered the joys of boomerang throwing, it's time to share that interest with others. Clubs and competitions are a great outlet for learning tips from other throwers, sharpening your accuracy and speed, and networking. Boomerang throwing doesn't just have to be a solitary hobby; if you want to put the time into it, throwing can also be a competitive sport. In this chapter, you'll learn how to connect with your local boomerang club, which may be the next step in improving your skills so that you can enter your first competition.

Boomerang Clubs

You don't need advanced skills to join a local boomerang club. Perhaps you can get some helpful pointers from the more advanced throwers. Check out your local newspaper's activities section to see if there are any boomerang clubs in your area or contact a national boomerang organization. They will help you find the nearest club. You can contact your state's chapter of the United States Boomerang Association (USBA).

If you don't live in the United States, you can check on the International Federation of Boomerang Associations (IFBA) website to see if your country has a national boomerang club. An early form of the worldwide organization started in 1991 and continued to grow. It evolved into its present form in 2003. This world union comprises associations from Australia, Brazil, the Czech Republic, France, Germany, Italy, Japan, Pakistan, Switzerland, the United Kingdom, and the United States. (See the websites for the USBA and the IFBA listed on page 46.)

You can always start your own informal group of boomerang enthusiasts. You can meet up every weekend and take turns throwing in a nearby field. Eventually, you may have people at different levels, so the more advanced ones can help beginners who are new to the group.

Participating in a chapter of your country's boomerang association, such as the USBA, is a great way to connect with other athletes who care about the sport. Founded in 1980, the USBA is a nonprofit organization dedicated to furthering many different aspects of the sport, from competitions to advances in science and also the craft of making boomerangs.

One of the many events that USBA helps organize is Toss Across America, which is an annual boomerang event for the general public that is held simultaneously in areas around the United States. Local experts partner with the USBA to create activities that teach people how a boomerang works and the skills and craftsmanship involved in throwing and making boomerangs.

Boomerang Competitions

Boomerang throwers can test their skills in accuracy, distance, catching, and maximum time aloft in several competition events both as individuals and as team players. Here are the most well-known ones, which are featured in national competitions and in the World Boomerang Championship.

Individual Events

As a beginner, you're probably thinking it's hard enough to complete a perfect throw and catch. Can you imagine trying to catch your boomerang as many times as you can in five minutes? At first, that might sound easy enough to do, but you also have to deal with the changing wind, precision of your throws and catches, and fatigue. Once you're more comfortable with your throwing and catching skills, perhaps you'll be inspired to practice a few of these events.

Accuracy: The goal is to throw your boomerang from a 2-meter-wide (about six and a half feet wide) center circle and score points based on how close it lands to the center circle. There are five concentric circles painted on the ground with the point values spaced 2 meters (about six and a half feet) apart. The points range from 10 points for a landing in the innermost circle to 1 point for a landing in the outermost circle. If your boomerang lands on the line between two circles, then the judges split the difference. Your boomerang must remain untouched during its return. You're allowed five throws. Each throw must travel at least 20 meters (more than 65 feet). The best score for a round is 50 points. (In Accuracy 100, you're allowed ten throws, which yields more consistent results than regular Accuracy.) The best type of boomerang for this event would be a dense one so that it doesn't land too far from the center circle.

Maximum Time Aloft (MTA): For this event, you should use a specially designed MTA boomerang, such as a lightweight one made of carbon fiber. You want to keep your boomerang hovering in the air as long as possible before you catch it within the competition circle. The time will only count if you catch it. You can make five throws, and your best time will count. Boomerangs can stay aloft anywhere between 25 seconds to over a minute. For the MTA 100, the competition circle has a diameter of 100 meters (about 328 feet). The problem is that sometimes your boomerang will drift with the wind, so you might have to run from the diameter of the circle to catch up with it. In MTA Unlimited, you're allowed to throw and catch anywhere on the field.

Fast Catch: In this event, you try to get the fastest time for five catches. Throwing takes place in the center circle, but catching can happen anywhere in the area. Your boomerang must travel at least 20 meters (more than 65 feet). Your time is recorded after you've made your last catch and touched the center circle. The time limit is about one minute.

Endurance: How many catches can you make in five minutes? This is basically Fast Catch but with a five-minute time limit. How long can you last? Hopefully, the wind will cooperate and not change too much during those five minutes. Again, you're throwing from the center circle with throws that travel at least 20 meters (more than 65 feet). This event takes stamina, focus, and steady catching.

Trick Catch/Doubling: Here's your chance to show your flexibility and creative catching. In the first part of this event, you're given a sequence of ten catches, which vary in difficulty and point value. You make the throws from the center circle. The boomerang must travel 20 meters (more than 65 feet).

Singles

> **2 points: Left-hand clean** (catch with left hand)
>
> **2 points: Right-hand clean**
>
> **3 points: Two-hand-behind-the-back**
>
> **3 points: Two-hand-under-the-leg**
>
> **4 points: Eagle catch** (like an eagle, you dive onto your boomerang from above and make a one-handed catch)
>
> **6 points: Foot hacky** (you kick your boomerang up like a hacky sack and then catch it)
>
> **6 points: Tunnel catch** (one- or two-handed catch under your leg with your feet planted on the ground)
>
> **7 points: One-hand-under-the-leg**
>
> **7 points: One-hand-behind-the-back**
>
> **10 points: Foot catch**

Guinness World Distance Record

The holder of the Guinness World Record for the longest throw of an object is Australian champion thrower David Schummy, with a throw of 1,401.5 feet (427.2 meters), which he made on March 15, 2005.

The second part of the event is called "doubling." The tricky part is that now you must throw two boomerangs simultaneously with one hand and then make two different catches. You have to hold the first boomerang while you catch the second one. You're given a pair of catches, but the order is up to you. If either one of your throws is short of 20 meters (more than 65 feet), you get a zero for the round.

Doubles
Two-hand-behind-the-back (3 points) and **two-hand-under-the-leg** (3 points)
Foot hacky (6 points) and **left-hand clean** (2 points)
Tunnel catch (6 points) and **right-hand clean** (2 points)
One-hand-behind-the-back (7 points) and **one-hand-under-the-leg** (7 points)
Foot catch (10 points) and **eagle catch** (4 points)

A throw-off is held if there are two or more throwers who scored perfect rounds. Athletes throw a sequence of two singles and two doubles simultaneously from different center circles. If you miss a catch, you're eliminated and the other throwers continue until there is one winner.

Throw-off
Tunnel catch (6 points)
Foot hacky (6 points)
One-hand-behind-the-back (7 points) and **one-hand-under-the-leg** (7 points)
Foot catch (10 points) and **eagle catch** (4 points)

Australian (Aussie) Round: This is one of the most difficult events, since you need to focus on achieving maximum distance and accuracy along with precise catching. You get to make five throws. All throws must be at least 20 meters (more than 65 feet), but you can get extra points for throws that go farther than that. A range of 2 to 6 points is possible for a boomerang that has a distance of 30 to 50 meters (98 to 164 feet). You can get 4 points for catching and a range of 10 to 1 points for accuracy. However, you can only get distance points if you successfully complete accuracy and catching. Here's an ideal throw: your boomerang zips 50 meters/164 feet (6 points) and you make a great catch (4 points) while in the center circle (10 points). To achieve a perfect round, you would do this five times to score a total of 100 points.

Here's something to keep in mind for accuracy points: higher values of points are awarded to locations that are closer to the center circle. This means that you can move, or even jump, toward the center circle while making a catch. Another strategy would be to reach out as far as you can to catch your boomerang while your foot stays near the center circle.

Tip for Airplane Travel

When traveling on an airplane to a competition, bring your boomerangs with you in a carry-on bag, since their wings are fragile. It's not on the prohibited list, so most airport security shouldn't give you any trouble about this. A boomerang is just another piece of sporting equipment. In comparison, a tennis racquet is larger, and it's allowed as a carry-on.

Team Events

There are two types of team events. They can either be fashioned after individual events with one person from each team throwing simultaneously or they can be group events with team members participating at the same time. The team versions of Accuracy, Aussie Round, MTA, and Trick Catch have similar rules to the individual events. For each event, two sets of two throwers represent each team. To get the team's total score, the judges add up the four individual scores. Group events like Team Supercatch, the Endurance Relay, and the Thirty-Meter Relay test teammates' speed, as well as their individual throwing and catching skills.

Team Accuracy: While standing in the center circle, the two team players must throw their boomerangs timed at about three seconds apart. If their boomerangs collide, both players get a score of zero.

Team Aussie Round: Like in Team Accuracy, the two team players launch their boomerangs from the center circle timed at about three seconds apart. Like the individual event, the players continue to make four more throws.

Team Maximum Time Aloft (MTA): This plays out the same way as the individual event. The team's total score is the combination of the team players' individual scores.

Team Supercatch: This team event is a cross between Fast Catch and MTA. One player makes an MTA throw. While that player's boomerang is in the air, the other three teammates must complete as many fast catches as they can. Their score is equal to the total number of fast catches. The team gets a score of zero if the MTA drops.

Endurance Relay: The four team players take turns throwing and catching their boomerangs in the center circle for one minute. The first player must sprint 20 meters (more than 65 feet) to the center circle and has one minute to achieve the highest amount of throws and catches possible. When the time is up, that player sprints back and tags the second player. This continues until all four players have performed their throws and catches. If there is any extra time, one of the players (usually the first player) goes back into the center circle to make more throws and catches.

30-Meter (about 98 feet) Relay: Four team players take turns sprinting 30 meters to the center circle. The first player sprints 30 meters to the center circle, throws the boomerang 30 meters, and catches it as quickly as possible. The player then sprints back and tags the second player. Each player will go into the center circle twice. The score is calculated by adding up the individual split times (the time between tags).

Team Trick Catch/Doubling: The scoring rules are the same as the individual event. The first team player makes the throw and catch followed by a teammate who must throw and perform the same catch in 15 seconds. Their scores are combined to calculate the team's total score.

World Boomerang Championship

The highest level of international competition for nationally ranked boomerang throwers is the World Boomerang Championship. It has been held every two years in a different host country since 1987. In 2010, the World Championship was in Rome, Italy. In 2012, it will be held in São Paulo, Brazil. The winning team is the keeper of the trophy until the next World Championship.

The winning team in 2010 was Rad Revolution from the United States. Team members included twin brothers Daniel and Richard Bower, Billy Brazelton, Logan Broadbent, Matt Golenor, Dan Johnson, and Gregg Snouffer. (The German team B-Motions had won the last three World Championships in 2004, 2006, and 2008.) Manuel Schuetz from Switzerland won the title of "World Long Distance Champion" with a throw of 176 meters (more than 577 feet). Alex Opri from Germany became the new world boomerang champion in the individual event.

There were twenty teams from Australia, Brazil, France, Germany, Italy, Japan, Switzerland, and the United States, as well as three other teams: international, veterans, and women's international. In 2010, countries were able to send as many as three teams; usually the number is two teams. In the individual events, there were players from Australia, Brazil, Bulgaria, the Czech Republic, Denmark, Finland, France, Germany, Holland, Italy, Japan, Spain, Switzerland, and the United States.

Team Selection

In order to become a member of the U.S. team for the World Championship, an athlete must qualify in the top twenty-four rankings in the national system. The athlete would also have to have participated in a minimum of three tournaments that year. The USBA invites 18 to 24 people to a three-day simulation tournament, which is held in early October or November. U.S. team members are selected based on their performance in this tournament. Two teams with six members each are created. The top four finishers pick the next two players for their team. Then the next four highest finishing throwers pick two more to fill their squad.

Women and the Sport

The boomerang sport continues to grow and more women are participating. At the 2010 World Championship, the international women's team participated as in past years, but there was also the first all-women's team from France.

Betsylew Miale-Gix has been a trailblazer for women in boomerang throwing. For five World Championship competitions, she was the only woman on the U.S. team, and she has participated since 1998. She is a five-time women's individual world champion. In 2008, she broke the world record for unlimited time aloft when she kept her boomerang in the air for 3 minutes and 49 seconds. This marked the first time a woman had set the world record for MTA. When asked about what drew her to the sport as a female athlete, she replied, "Boomerang throwing is one of the few sports where men and women can compete equally, which is exciting and fulfilling. A woman can compete with a man if she's willing to work hard enough and has the talent to do it." Today's female competitors continue to push the sport of boomerang throwing to higher levels of excellence.

The Future of the Sport

Competitions are also a great way for the general public to gain exposure to the sport. Boomerang throwing may not ever have as much recognition as other sports with individual and team events like swimming and track and field (in particular, the individual and relay races). But through events like Toss Across America and the World Boomerang Championship, in the public eye it's gaining more respect as a competitive sport. Individual and team events require precision, agility, and speed. Disciplined athletes strive to break world records. Who knows? Maybe one day boomerang throwing will become an Olympic event.

CONCLUSION
A Growing Community

Boomerang throwing has expanded from a local pastime to a worldwide community. There are enthusiasts who enjoy crafting boomerangs while there are others who enjoy competitions. And there's plenty of room for more throwers.

You don't have to just practice alone. If you want to share your passion for the sport with others, you can join the larger boomerang community. Get involved in your local club, start your own informal group, or sign up for a competition. You and your fellow throwers can also do a demonstration at a local school or in your hometown.

If you want to improve your technique or learn more about competition events, there are lots of great websites in the next section of this book. You can read up on the latest world records, watch videos of trick catching, or chat with other throwers on message boards.

At the end of the day, what matters most is the satisfaction that comes from throwing your boomerang. You connect with your boomerang. Then, with a snap of your wrist, it's spinning away from your hand. Even though you've launched your boomerang hundreds of times, you still watch in awe as it gracefully loops through the air.

Out there on the field, it's just you, your boomerang, and the wind. You learn to stay attuned to your environment and make adjustments to your technique. With plenty of practice, you gain an instinct, almost a sixth sense, in what to do.

On those tough days when nothing seems to be going right, just keep practicing. Remember to adapt to the wind's direction and add plenty of spin.

Now go out there and have some fun!

WEBSITES

Boomerang Association of Australia
www.boomerang.org.au
Explore this website's extensive glossary of boomerang terms.

The Boomerang Man
www.theboomerangman.com
This vendor sells more than twenty different brands of boomerangs, including left-handed boomerangs.

Boomerang News
www.boomnews.net
Here you'll find the latest boomerang topics that are available on the Internet.

Boomerang USA
www.usba.org/boomerangusa.org
Learn information on competitions and national rankings.

Boomerang World
www.flight-toys.com/boomerangs.htm
This website features an extensive list of links on many topics, including vendors, clubs, science, history, and kid-friendly throwing instructions. If you're shopping for a boomerang, check out the Flight-Toys Boomerang Catalog.

Boomerangs.org
www.boomerangs.org
Explore a variety of topics, including how to throw a boomerang, and clubs and organizations.

Boomerangs.TV

www.boomerangs.tv

Check out some great videos of world champions in action.

Gel Boomerangs

www.gel-boomerang.com

There's a good article about how to throw in windy conditions on this website.

HowStuffWorks: How Boomerangs Work

www.howstuffworks.com/boomerang.htm

This website offers a solid explanation on the science behind a boomerang's flight. It also features helpful animated illustrations.

International Federation of Boomerang Associations

www.ifba-online.com

If you don't live in the United States, you can check to see if your country has a national boomerang club on this website. You can also find a link to the upcoming World Boomerang Championship website here.

United States Boomerang Association

www.usba.org

Read about membership in the USBA, find a boomerang vendor, or watch videos featuring world champions. Click on "The Sport" tab to get to a list of local USBA chapters.